AF413509

THE SIMPLEST THING

Also by Don Langford

In the Light of the Full Moon: Dispersions, Glimpses, and Reflections

Songs from Deep Time

Dwelling in the Twilight Realm

Water Rock Time

Fragrant Blossoms, Fading Light

Five Gates of Entry: Selected Poems

THE SIMPLEST THING

POEMS

Don Langford

Published by D S Langford Publishing
Columbus, OH 43229

Printed in the United States

Cover design by Don Langford,

Names: Langford, Don, author
Title: *The Simplest Thing* / Don Langford

ISBN 979-8-9910480-4-0 (hardback)
ISBN 979-8-9910480-5-7 (paperback)
ISBN 979-8-9910480-6-4 (ebook)

Library of Congress Control Number Pending

First Printing, February 2026

For Marlene

In spring sleep, dawn arrives unnoticed.
Suddenly, all around, I hear birds in song.
A loud night. Wind and rain came, tearing
blossoms down. Who knows few or many?

"Spring Dawn"
Meng Hao-jan (689-740)
trans. David Hinton

Contents

About the Author

Part 1

Early Lessons

The child plays
        with appearance and disappearance,
        with presence and absence

Waving hands and laughing
        in joyful play

Mother's face coming and going
        behind hands opening and closing

Spellbound child
        no language yet
        no explanations, no word traps

Like new each time,
        full of wonder

Something funny, wise child,
        about coming and going

Buoyancy

In the playground of my youth
children gathered round our trusting teacher
in a circle on the uncut clover-scented grass

There she invited me, the new arrival,
to join her inside the circle of my newest friends.

In that memory of smiling faces
my classmates gathered closely around me
and the teacher gently guided me back, and I leaned softly
       into a dozen warm and supporting arms
       as my feet lifted slowly above the ground,

          and floating like the clouds above me
          I did not know then that such safety
          and trust in those around me
          could ever evaporate in the mist
             of passing years.

All around the circle of clouds above me
the giggling faces of boys and girls,
their hands tightly clasped securely beneath my weightless body,
sharing their joy with me
in a timeless yet ordinary moment
on a warm spring afternoon
when our favorite teacher led us outside
into the sun where we laughed and learned
the best lessons of living.

Standing in Stillness

In the pool,
under water,
bubbles float up toward the sky,
bursting among the reflected clouds—

and shafts of sunlight
beam their jagged way in ripples
to the blue bottom where my feet
wave silently in their stillness.

The Simplest Thing

In a pool I asked a floating woman
how she did that without sinking
and she said it's the simplest
and most natural thing in the world;
then she bent her head back into the water
and spread her arms and legs
and soon she was resting there atop the water
like a contented starfish in the morning sun.

And in that clear blue mountain light
I could see that the secret
was to place the ears under water
and not listen to the noises from above,
allowing the gurgling from the depths
to be the music of this letting go.

Learning to Juggle

First, he said, start with one ball,
not a beanbag or tennis ball—
something solid to toss in the air
with one hand then the other
sometimes low, sometimes high.

Notice how to feel and control its location
            in the air;
learn the feeling of your curved fingers
            and the weight on your palms
            of the falling ball.

Then, toss it from one hand to the other
            and fling it high into the air.
When you can stop thinking about it,
            it's time to move on.

Pass the ball from one hand to the other
            and toss a second ball into the air;
            catch and toss them in four-four time,
            sometimes higher, sometimes lower,
            focusing without thinking.

Then toss the balls straight up, catching them
            in the same hand.
Practice daily for a month. No hurry—
            getting to thoughtless concentration.
Bounce a few off your head or the ceiling,
            then get back to business— juggling
            playfulness and work.

Learn to juggle in your sleep; move on to three balls
            in the air, cascading like water, flowing
            round and round in your hands automatically,
            while your mind moves with your hands and lilting body
                        in new refreshing rhythms.

Take it outside; try juggling the dogs and the daily news;
            throw a few subterranean anchors high into the sky,
            catch two clouds in one hand and let them go
                        to the surprised faces that you pass
                        without thought; return to the work of juggling
                        playfulness and focused concentration
                        in the weightlessness of your distant fingertips.

Mountain Lore

Along the mountain trail
        there is a tree
        --a large woody shrub really—
                growing out of solid rock
                through the thinnest broken crack

All the upward-climbing hikers
        grab hold of its brown-bark branches,
        trusting its tenacious grip;
        they see it as a sentinel on the wind-swept crag,
        an inspiration for their own ascent

With each tug on its waving branches
        the rock-bound shrub tightens its own grip
        to support the upward-bound climbers

Paraglider

Over distant sand dunes
        a blue and white sail appears,

            kite curving in air
                    bending, arcing
                    along the beach-line

            somewhere, invisible,
                    a marionette
                    alone but not lonely
                    plucks the delicate strings

Closer still,
            an acrobat in wind and sun
            races above windblown ocean waves

            skipping over sea notes
            in a ballerina jazz flow
            unfamiliar terrain, new sensations

Here is the lone artist
his windblown craft on display
            for anyone walking on the sand
            or for no audience at all

The paraglider is the air poet
            spinning, mute
            without fanfare
            writing his shifts and swirls above
                    the windblown waves

Season's End

After holding on tightly
through the long green summer
winds and rains,

in autumn, the apples fall easily
with the curled yellow leaves,

opening space between branches
for the sky to shine through

The Quiet Morning Air

In the morning silence
before the sun has baked
        the eastern walls,

before the dogs begin to yelp
and machines raise the dead
        in non-stop noise,

there is a quiet hope,
a sliver of potential,
a passing remembrance,
        a brief balance
        on the fulcrum

where love and kindness
        have a chance to dwell
        without falling
        off the shelf in ridicule

A temporary peace
rests quiet and clean,
fragile in its momentary stillness

This breath of secular purity
in the quiet morning air
is where I return,
as to the town's water well,
for daily restoration

Seeking Recognition

Outwardly, they are all sitting
        pensive and still
        in thought, perhaps in pain

        all forward facing

        posed for the camera
        of my memory

        frozen, stillness, a moment

        a lifetime picture-book of faces
        some wrinkled and sun-browned
        some alabaster white, some shiny black,
        eyes open, forward stillness

Faces with eyes weary or piercing,
        deep in thought or distant

        some tired

Haunted faces that hold me long,
some whimsical and unremarkable
        that fly by like a crowd

        all the faces concealing
        worlds that their own words
        cannot convey, nor mine

Their eyes pull me in
        to the surface of their papered faces

        unable to penetrate or explore

        My face presses to theirs;
        caves with entrances

into mystery and connection

        in darkness, closed to my pleadings

Now, waking from my reverie,
I sit before a torrent of passing people

      glimpsing their picture-book faces;
      they do not stare or peer into my eyes

I seek some sign of recognition
      and in their averted eyes
      the long forgetting is revealed

Along the Roadside

The late season mowing machines
have decapitated the roadside colors,
laid low the fragrant fields,
tamed the creepers and vines.

Signage and laws have pushed the hitchhikers, too,
     off the roadsides into town.

Years ago I picked up Whitey and Maryanne
     along the roadside
     outside Palm Springs,
     drove them four days;
     after luck-filled adventures, a quick goodbye,
     Calgary train yard to hop the freights.

Today the short-growing dandelions have learned
     to keep their heads low
     and push up their seed balloons
     the day after mowers pass,
     like mice after the cat retreats.

Uprooted and Wandering
(in memory of my father)

The deer, driven by fire,
moved deeper into the wood

In silence they lost their voices,
led their young by the sound
        of their hooves on leaves

We inhabited their land in the green wooded north,
then traveled south through scorched desert,
toward an oasis of comfort,

Like many others
we were overcome
by the drowsiness of culture

Only later we learned
we had been among the latest wave
of ignorant invaders on Turtle Island

The deer and their caretakers
had been driven into the distance
by men with fire in their eyes

The land of the caretakers
is now unrecognizable
and today we long for the deer
        and quietness of the north

Connected

You turned the page
and here you are
in touch for just this moment
with someone at the other end
          of these words

in so many ways
          like the smiles
          of those you glimpsed
          yesterday

the briefest intersection
          so easy to ignore
          as inconsequential.

And from the words and smiles
perhaps an embrace,
the memory of a heartfelt pulling-in—

Or the recollection
of some vanishing moments,
the forks in the road,
the impulsive decisions
that led you to where you are.

Accumulated glimpses
spawned by these words on a page
from someone you may never meet,

but a fellow companion nevertheless,
reaching out to you with language,
traveling with you for a time
in the same direction.

Waiting Room

Across the small room her casual smile,
unforced and gentle, broke through
all my world-weary resistance to passion.
I turned around to see if it was meant for someone else,
but her soft smile persisted when my gaze
again returned to her. I did not stare and began to feel
the weight of her unwavering grin, softer than words.

I did not want to be let down again
and learn that something menacing and frightful
was about to happen like the premonition of a raging fire
that she had started, or a nest of spiders descending upon my head.
Then again, maybe she was listening to some pleasant music
or remembering good news about a loved one
cured by modern medicine.

I occupied myself with the folds in my trousers,
the way the material draped in a smooth curve
over my knee. I listened to the office girls talking about
a television show they had watched the night before.
When I turned my head back again, the smile
seemed more intense, definitely intended for me,
pulling at me magnetically, but I resisted getting up and
crossing the room to embrace her and to ask
where she had been and how had she been living
all these years. We had lifetimes to catch up on,
but I looked away again, inspecting my fingernails
and feeling the heat rising on my face.

How long this continued, I don't recall.
I honestly don't even know how it ended; I may have
been called in to see the doctor, or I may have briefly
dozed off until she had gone. Perhaps she was called in
to see a specialist, or her husband had come out
with a good prognosis.

There was, I now recall, the brief moment of an empty chair,
then the next moment an elderly woman was sitting there
with the largest beatific smile I have ever seen, directed
right at me.

Soft and unimposing, but striking and inviting me
to drop my guard and make an effort to return a smile

now and then, from the heart, with sincere affection
without any demands or expectations, knowing
that our short time together in this waiting room
is where the real healing occurs.

Mining the Moon

The outer surface of the bright full moon
and all its shimmering reflections
on lakes, in hearts,
spawned a million romantic poems

The wisest among us
drew inspiration
from the magisterial
fullness and mystery
of its monthly return

Curiosity and speculation
yielded to exploration
and discovery,
probing beneath the footprints
into veins of ore

Through magnified lenses
commoners now view
lunar factories
transforming centuries of dreams
into landscapes of industry,
blinding the dreamy eyes of wonder

The Art of No Thing

Wizened one, old poet,
casting your warning windward,
"Usura rusteth the chisel
It rusteth the craft and the craftsman"

You speak to me, a word-weary bystander
resting on the roadside, late bloomer
dusted under foot by a brigade of boomers

Down the road
a young burning candle
offers up a guiding light:
"In my craft and sullen art"
he booms and echoes,
and I, with words yet to share,
do certainly write for those
"who pay no praise of wages
nor heed my craft or art,"
and I cast my lines into the dark abyss
where depth and distance
find no reward but in the beauty
            of their silence

Neither do I step into the road
and join the parade of poets;
these few books in my satchel
do not weigh me down, their pleasurable burden
I carry alone to the end of the day
where I practice the dying art of no thing,
no books to peddle, nor beggar to feed,
a few pounds left on these weary bones

Parler depuis la Tombe

Into the Berkeley hills
we took our basket of raviolis chauds,
Gruyère, Cabernet, et olives noires;
we spread our quilted blanket, and
over the rooftops below, we imagined
a glittering blue Mediterranean
dans le lointain

That was many years ago,
when President Marcus Aurelius and Leonardo,
the nation's health secretary, dispensed wisdom
and the best in science and arts

We were cradled in peace
resting carefree on our summer blanket
l'innocence de la jeunesse
eucalyptus trees redolent
in their aromatic green

You spread sprigs of fragrant rosemary
je me souviens bien;
it was a time of pleasure and light
long before the plague of avarice and greed
forced its menacing grip into our lives;
long before les temps sombres des assassinats
and state-imposed poverty,
when we still had our books of poetry
and glimpsed a flourishing moment of Florentine art
in our own fast-moving Renaissance

For years after, we carried with us
the long road of good fortune into the approaching night.
In resistance, artists and farmers and laborers
carried a common banner against the rising tyranny,
and for a time it seemed that anything was possible.
Those were the days, my friend.

Nightfall

this evening's diaphanous sunset
        smeared cloudless
        across the horizon

the color of plum flesh
        drifting to blue

        to distant rain black
        at nightfall

reports of ice and rain
        where home once was
        far away

cold winter there
        open windows here

today I read history
        of Mexico
        outdoors
        in breezy warm shade

thinking too of family
        no longer living

Stepped inside
        closed windows, sat in warm light

        out there, unseen,
        night moves westward

Cool Desert Breeze

Is it enough to feel the cool breezes,
to find contentedness walking
in the foothills,
       no longer climbing to the heights

The desert is a good place to find one's limits
      and still be rewarded
      with sunset spreading colors
      over the canyons

Here the leafy shrubs wave and bend in the wind
      the Saguaro strong and straight
      coyotes call together in the night
      when it is their time to shout their wildness

Even the mighty pines recognize
      the law of the treeline
      and the wolves, too, climb no higher

Before Sunset

Sea bird in flight
        beady eye downward,
        its fish-filled beak
        clenched in flapping fog

There is no thunder
        nor windy snow
        along the foamy shoreline

No filigreed troops
        marching on the drifting sands
        no pike-adorned heads
        with droopy-eyed stares

Then why we sit clutching knees
        without a blanket to save us
        from the dumb mid-day foam
        ebbing feet-ward?

Passions blowing in green swirls
        not a rock cliff in sight
        the beach line smooth as a palm
        extended as proof or promise

The sun-welcoming horizon
        is hidden far in the filtered whiteness
        blinding any clear view
        of mute blue sea nymphs

Our afternoons float
        beyond the oblivion of night's dreams
        in cold wet numbness
        knowing the sun will fall
        when the horizon pulls it to its golden knees

Eyes of Wonder

The eyes of chimpanzee, dog—and infant in the pram—
     look with attentive wonder.

How like the recognition we feel
     in unguarded moments,

caught staring and grinning for no reason
     other than for the pure pleasure
     of experiencing wonder, the special glimpse.

But for us, the wondrous veil drops, through our long learning,
     yet we recognize something remote and distant
     in those innocent eyes reminding us
        of possibilities, and a longing.

Dream Home

Imagined mind, roaming into ancient China mountains,
       misty gray in green tree canopy
       a mental painting, repeated for years, like memory

Foot-worn path through wooded thicket
       alongside curving river water,
       large rounded stones glistening

Small cottage, thatched roof,
       birds and flowers, sun and rain,
       small garden, greens for soup

I am not in this picture,
       always seen from a distance;
       the scent of smoke from a neighbour's hut
       unseen in the private distance

Imagined mind, gently longing
       for resting place with quiet friendly neighbour
       near enough to walk for talk and tea
       far enough for snow-silent winters

Part 2

Canker at the Flower Tip

While our eyes were averted, it seems,
the days grew harder, darker,
the old neighbour no longer leaned
        in friendly chat at the window sill
        in common shirtsleeves, sharing views
                and news of family
                or the cost of food and sundries

something coarse and quick
        in our neighbour's voice
        called children in from their daily play
                in the once-wild streets

As if overnight, they recoiled and pulled their shutters closed,
        the neighbourhood grew more brittle and cold,
        bitterness flared in suspicious stares
        while words were guarded, accents controlled

Old friendly gates swung closed;
        the nation's flowers grew cankerous with rot at the top,
        a toxic smell of poison in the air

The protectors fled in silence
        and packs of wolves
        carried off our neighbours
        one by one
        in the dark of night—
        disappeared into faraway lands

The screams of torture broke into our dreams
        as the pain came closer in
        and again the band played on
        blaring music through the air,
        broadcasters entertaining in distracting sport

In uneasy silence we listened
        for the screams to subside
        but they only grew louder,

Until finally, people gathered in the streets,
        of necessity again, to ask
        what have we become

And in solidarity we began to shout
          with louder voices still,
          what needed to be done
          to call for civility and freedom
                    to return home again

From the Ruins of Andriivka

How far into Avidya?
        Farther still to Andriivka—
        heart and home of a generation,
        blue sky over wheat field flags,
        a graveyard in ruins

Children's hollow stares, blank
        with loss of fathers
        and grieving mothers

How to give birth again to compassion?
        Harder still to soothe the hatreds
        that breed for lifetimes
        from war with no victors

Far away, talk of peace comes easily,
        remote innocence, ignorance
        deluded in comfort, antidote
        for hopeless cynicism

It is the simplest thing
        to close one's eyes
        refuse to see,
        avoid inquiring
        and asking why

Harder still, to stop the wars
        that many endure
        while others wade deep
        into the waters of Lethe

We Watched the Taming

We watched the wild horses across Nevada's open range-land,
packs of survivors, sleek coats, finding the hidden water sources,
eating the scrub, mating and caring for their young,
teaching generations to survive.
We watched them roaming.

We watched the fence posts piled high,
the post-hole diggers positioned
and holes neatly spaced in long curving lines.
We watched the corrals constructed, then the dust rising.

We watched the wild horses herded,
panic in their bulging fiery eyes;
they kicked and bucked, feeling rope for the first time,
a strange strangulation squeezing their wild spirit.

They stomped wildly in their logged pens,
dizzy with rage, exhausting themselves
day after day, fenced in the hot sun;
We watched them tire and learn to walk in circles.

We watched from our own place of acceptance,
knowing the reasons why we watched,
understanding how easy it is to lose the wildness—
the ease of losing the will to kick against the sky.

Turning Point

Well into the play
the actors turned their backs
            to the audience.

Tattered clothing fell to the floor
            exposing bare bloodied legs
            amid bellicose cries

The descending curtain
            revealed blackened feet
            shuffling stage right.

Had the forward momentum
            of the action halted

or was this, too, part of what
            the script had suggested?

Could mutiny be possible
            in the assignments
            we were given?

Could we say in the mid-scene of our lives
            we will alter the script
            and honor war no more

or manufacture the bombs
            that fall on our neighbours,
            incinerating the villages we visited
            only yesterday?

The stage lights dim, then grow darker still
            as janitors sweep the floor,
            and in the dark and silent hall
            we draft again tomorrow's closing scene.

Field Hospital

We settled into our daily comforts
        blankets pulled tightly to our chins
        calling for sleep to come to these wide eyes
        explosions still fresh in our bones

The skin burns for change
        here in the depths of our healing
        beds of tourniquets and iodine
        bandaged legs pointing up

The smell of dying never washes away
        time stops in the darkened corners
        the nurse's cool fingers feel close to heaven
        for one who clings to the narrow thread

In the still real realm of the living
        we breathe the sweet safe air
        never knowing when the valve turns tight
        and the folded window cloth is darkened

Blind Injustice

For eyes that do not see
       beyond the near horizon
       nor beyond today

the milky green morning
       portends darker miseries
       never felt before

The ruminations are a taste of fortunes
       yet to come for some
       like dreams foretold,
       or nightmares still unfolding

The simple dreary colors
       a walkway of cobbled stone
       marshaled into hastened order
       though hurricanes wash them all away

With our senses all aglow
       waiting, anxious, flowing cold,
       the mighty strains do unfold
       in languid mourning

In the snapping judgment air
       the courts will rule afoul
       sending freedom to the wall
       and justice to the hanging pole

Illusoriness of Islands

What is an island
but a momentary presence

in a chain of mountains
not yet submerged
by the rising and ebbing

of oceans,
themselves ever displaced

in rising land surfaces
and water escaping into air.

There is no isolated self
in the ocean of webbed connections;

only illusory separateness
hidden among mountains,
valleys, water, and air.

The Season of Pruning Nears

This adopted state is grieving,
infected by sickness, a canker
budding in its uppermost branches

deformities and blighted leaves abound;
a pungent odor warns.

Birds from valleys and mountains near and far
no longer come; we miss their plumage colors;
they do not add their wondrous song
to the chorus now grown quiet
with poison-scented perfume hanging
amid the twisted branches.

In this temporary contagion
the birds seek harbor in distant places,
finding food and shelter, safety for their young.

The season of pruning nears,
protecting the strong persisting roots,
lopping off the toxic limbs,
snipping away the yellow curled leaves,
stimulating a new generation of healthy growth
so the birds with their songs return again.

Such trees do not thrive in isolation;
they rely upon the grove.
As the season of pruning nears
the distant birds are waiting;
       their patient plumage grows.

The Veil of Intuition

Sitting in silence I listen to a chorus of voices
            in my head

They spin out fragments in different tones
at first inflecting wordy pairs and triads
in such rapid succession that I do not know
how many there are speaking so incessantly
            competing for my attention

So I stare and wait
confident that the chorus will settle
following my calm example
and in due course one non-corporeal voice advances
inclined by intuition or by the Muse
quietly working behind the scenes

A simple phrase rises quietly at first,
            then repeats and refines
            becoming something unanticipated
            known only to the silent domain
            that does not sit for interview

The phrase or vision stands before me
            with assurance that there is more to follow
            if only I place it on a page
            where sluice gates open
            for the pouring out
            of words in orderly persuasion
            resting on the page

From trance-like silence ideas form
            and when the spell finally inclines toward the edit
            I dip my bucket deep into the well of gratitude
            for allowing me to brush again
                  against the veil of intuition

A Little Ink Spot

This same simple story
told a thousand times
to nods and conversation;
at times, deep contemplation.

A life, near idyllic in early years
turns in later to pain and suffering

tendons tighten and back hunches forward;
the muscles storing increments of trauma
curl like autumn leaves.

They say the eyes remain unchanged, but
from outside they do not see the glaucoma glaze
        or sclerotic pipes and tubes inside,
            the mind closing in on wayward thoughts
                and voices from deep inside

The story runs from one's own gains
            to outward concerns
            to the difficulties of others
            the entanglements of age
            the creeping misalignments
            the malignant eruptions and cankers
                appearing abruptly during the night

The glimpse is not a story
the fool is not a king
but sandy beaches were once mountains
wind and tides shaped their fate

the windswept pines, strong and mute, only glimpse the story
            and we sit with our little sorrows
            here today and gone tomorrow;
                a little ink spot upon the page,
                nowhere near the story being told.

Up in Flames

The dream resembled the memory,
       muted teacup shards angled in ash mud,
       a brick fireplace smoldering in sunlight;
       the stench of an incinerated world melted and glazed;
       a passing flash of what it looked like two days before
       when pine-scented mountains welcomed the day.

The dream resembled the memory,
       the gate swung out onto a grassy lane;
       the hum of insects in the sweet prairie morning;
       the creaking of ice-coated birch trees in winter;
       summer friends and neighbours stopping by.

The dream resembled the memory,
       before the cords were severed,
       before the dreams turned dark and cold
       when fear invaded the hearts of neighbours;
       then hoarfrost lost its beauty.

The dream resembled the memory
       when children dreamed of a future.
The dream resembled the memory
       until we analyzed it closely.
The dream resembled the memory,
       fragments burning up in flames;
       hopes imploding into deep sonorous tones
              of life's forgotten memories
              seeking solace in the escape of dreams,
              imploring the night to be kinder tomorrow;
              forgetting it all in a numb and saddened stare.

Figments of Fear

The wind howled loudly last night,
deep and hollow, a bewildering force
to pull our little world apart.

Were such wild winds that blow eternally
really the source of phantoms
       for our ancestors
       who huddled wide-eyed
       in the night

painting space creatures on cave walls,
       aiming their harpoons
       at giant predators?

What will be our superstitions, cataloged
by future historians, as the phantasms
we blamed on adversaries or mental figments?

A long list of imagined fictions to rally
       a threatened population
       honing the skills and instruments of war
       in superstitious fear.

Just think of all the frightful abominations
       that erupted out of distant days
       of childhood innocence,

       and even those who would save us
       from eternal winds and fires;

       yes, especially the saviors
       claiming to protect us,
       who would become abominations
       to their victims.

Witness the Fall

The messenger, his steaming horse frothing,
dismounted and delivered the welcomed code,
The hasp is off the gate.

The fate of kings and pretenders,
inglorious fall from the heights of hubris

Watch the supplicants writhe in pain,
        squirming like snakes
        in the pit of their undoing

They will molt and wonder
what colors shall they wear,
like chameleon clowns stumbling over themselves

We waken from our long soft slumber
to an emerging understanding—
we live in historic times,
a different act in the same captivating play
rehearsed a thousand times in variation

Nature's law, cloaked in mystery:
what rises most certainly will fall

Witness the caving in,
the house of cards tumbling,
the king's court scattering like frightened mice,
the escape routes in the wainscoting
bunged shut, voices shouting, "Checkmate"

So much damage done when the cyclone is over.
Not all can be restored.

But the mending begins until the next assault,
and messengers feed the tired horses.

Still Life

Yes, there is a vase of flowers
centered on the table,
but I do not write of flowers today
or for any foreseeable day hereafter,

except to note that they are lavender violets
to mark the memory of friends unknown,
            friends I will not see or meet,

killed in resisting the haunting boot
            stomping on the face of freedom.

There is too much war and violence
to write about flowers and smiles today

except to note the innocence of smiling children
who convince us they represent a new future.

But if they live long enough
they, too, will be criticized by their youngers
for their own complacence and softness,
            when strength is desired.

The flowers will wilt, but the table that holds them
in their vases, will be passed from generation
to generation, supporting the colorful transient flashes
            that catch the passing eye.

The daily delights and laughter will snare the prize,
but the supporting table, darkened wood carved
by craftsman's chisel or lathe, rests quietly and still;
            the mute and solid support
            that holds the flowers, poems, and plays.

Flapping Sounds

Doors opening and closing,
so many they flapped
like bats at sunset
flowing from a darkened cave

It was the howling wind
that made them flap
so ominously, blackness
in that flattened sound

then a drumming pulse
inside my head

In this little cell
I will twirl about
flapping my arms
not to entertain
but to grow some wings
short and stubbed
folded tight and closely held
in the constant whirl

They will extend in time
these matted wings
a bee, a bird, just a being
unfolding in a cell, not a perch
or open field to look upon

When I whirl and kick,
the maddened gestures
break such tiny holes
in the edges of my confinement

When I peer into a different space,
looking out or deeper in,
the escape route is just a loop
back to the bed and cell
where I began

Where I fumble, fall,
and find my knees
scraping on the cobblestones,
and my eyes grown bleary,

wings with five fingers
writing letters on a wall

These are the little findings
in the morning air, incessant
flapping, seeking flight,
taking soundings in the final darkness,
finding refuge in the creases
of these broken wings
tightly folded in a cell

Ebb and Flow

At the water's edge
signs are posted, warning
against godless bliss
and contaminated fish;
against colors, umbrellas, and balloons

Posted threats against singing
generate wild hoots, rainbow dresses,
and painted faces

Sentries posted, bullhorns blaring,
drowned out by kazoos and laughter

In the ebb and flow of generations,
repression and jubilation alternated;
first the fist, and then embraces,
smiles concealed beneath the frowns

When both sides play the clowns,
at times free atop the world,
then later warring underground;

Come to the water's edge to see
if polluted waters evaporate,
or if colored balloons reach the moon

Auto Accident

Out of hot delirium
worlds unfold
tumbling forth, cascading

continents swimming
in a drop of water
through prisms of revolving light

the constant churning nebulae
contained just long enough
            to steal a glimpse of order
            before the windows close

Make no sense of these fiery glimpses
            with water-dampened eyes

All the order melts in time,
this the pattern of cars colliding

Larger scenes are still unwinding
when stars awaken to their fate
and in the farther sunlit fields
beyond the bandaged hallways
            and safety of the gauze
rooms open into other rooms
            of abandoned understanding

When delusions tumble forth
            in spiteful abundance,
            cleaving to old memories
            that float unobstructed
            long before speech returns,
            the nursemaid will cleanse your wounds

and through the throbbing incoherent words
            liquid soothing in the veins
            sweet elixir for cool delirium

Welcome to the end of dreams and lucky you
            if this ends well; beware the hellish road ahead
            remember first to say goodbye
            with sister morphine at the wheel

Drifting

The clouds never seemed out of focus
on those days without glasses

outdoors, looking up beyond
the daily news, half blind and hoping

the linkages of days, forming chain or net,
appearing enough like order

in the not-too-strange sea of images
finding some room for agreement

seeing different waves
in the same strange sea

along the sun-drenched beaches
party blankets, wistful kites resting,

a thousand different reasons
drawing us to breaking waves and sandy sun

seagulls and sand crabs intersecting
the lives of peopled visitors

and above, the clouds moved on,
reshaping wind and tide in shadow

Open Hand Poem

The gesture
        of open hand extended,
        palm upward;

An offering, the eyes confirm,
        a way of giving;

a sacral sharing in this safe place.

The poem, too, extends its openness—
        words like lotus blooms
        open on placid lake,
        or gentle voice
        confirming care
        in times of doubt

the warm embrace of words,
a comfort and balm to ease the hurt
        and hardness that comes with living.

An abiding strength
        in the motion of softness
        as water transforms the hardened stone
        in its gentle persistence,
        the poem's words repeated
        offer a song in healing gesture
                to open hearts
                in their receptive preparation

Page to Reader

If I could lift you up from here

I would,
if you desire,
        place you on the safest ground
        where you could begin anew

        or continue from where you are

If you see the power in words,
then all beneficence to you, dear reader,

May you be guided by peace on your journey,
[all this from a single poem in a little book]

It speaks to you, this little page,
a safe companion composed of words

to ask you to look up from this page
for just a moment and take notice of what you see;
scan the scene with gratitude
        and wonder

Gazing outward, hear these words and see their power
        within you:

        "It is really amazing that I am here at all."

See where you are and acknowledge this gratitude
        within you:

        the incredible odds that you are here—

reminded by a little poem on a page

Little Tide-Ridden Poem

Brightly colored pebbles in the cove

      on closer inspection
      smooth rounded glass
      broken bottles, tumbled by time

The way old poems, crafted and forgotten
      discovered anew

      distant, detached

      and farther still
      spun out like galaxies,
      telling their own stories

The sounds and shapes and colors
      forged in a moment long ago
      worn by wind and water and time

Held long in the sun, the pebbled poems
      lose their glint and sheen

In the wide expanse of rocky shoreline
      a little pebble here and there
      rolling in its dampened simplicity,
      tumbled in the temperament of incessant tides

Stay with Gratitude

Halfway across the roiling stream
       turning back, there's more to do

No need to retrace the way
       of old familiar footprints

There is time to see the fresh and new

green leafy branches
       mingle with memories of friends

the taste of summer berries
       inspiring a restful tune

waiting for humming
       with the birds
       that made it this far

So many species along the way
       that helped guide
       and frightened us into flight

Rest this weary thinking mind
       allow it to see in restful repose
       letting go and living fully
       for a time

there will be time for endings,
       but for now the smell of clover
       the sweet clover honey
       the buzz of bees
       the white boxes stacked
       the smoker ready at hand
       gratitude for the bee keeper
       and the farmer
       and the growers, the harvesters,
       and the children with their smiles

gratitude for the taste of living,
       the birdsong and the sun
       the turning seasons
       the animals and plants
           that share this time
           of being here with us

About the Author

Don Langford was born in Ontario, Canada, grew up in Southern California, and has lived in Oregon and Ohio. His most recent poetry collections include *Fragrant Blossoms, Fading Light* and *Five Gates of Entry: Selected Poems.* He spends his time writing, hiking, and traveling with his wife, Marlene.